Dublin Writers and their Haunts

Dublin Writers

and their Haunts

Written and Illustrated by SEÁN LENNON

First published 2003 by
FINGAL COUNTY COUNCIL
Dublin • Ireland
www.fingalcoco.ie

Copyright words and pictures © Seán Lennon, 2003

For Anne

ISBN 0 95266 545 X

ACKNOWLEDGEMENTS

The author would like to thank: the Fingal County Librarian, Paul Harris, for setting this project in motion and his remarkable support and encouragement every step of the way; the novelist, playwright and poet, Dermot Bolger, for his Foreword; the staff of Fingal Libraries and, in particular, the staff of Mobile Library including Anne Birch and Marjorie Sliney; Paul Doyle, Donncha O'Donnacdha, Seán Breen, Tony Carey and ... ry of Marino Library; Deirdre Ellis-King and the staff of Dublin City Libraries. While ... also became inde ... d to the following persons for their many kindnesses: Dan O'Donoghue, Paula How ... Naomi Moore, John Hackett, Declan Kiberd, Sinead O'Brien, Bernadette Bolger, Don C ... an Barry, Bob Gallico, Janine Gallico, Mike Birch, Quintin Roantree, Noel Costello, ... om Mullins, Seán McArdle, Ian Knox, Arja Kajermo, Peter Mooney, Seámus Dowlin ... heridan, Linda Longmore, Mary Donohue, Yvonne O'Brien, Yvonne McConville, and ... d Dermac Lennon, my most special people; Bill and Bob for working miracles; Maure ... to ... e, including a love of drawing – I know she would have liked these ones; Susan Wai ... n, to Paul Harris for his kind words and the publication of *Dublin Writers and their Ho ...*

This book is set in 13 on 16 point Dante

Designed by SUSAN WAINE *Printed in Ireland by* ßETAPRINT, DUBLIN

Contents

I am delighted to introduce Seán Lennon's latest book. The libraries department of Fingal County Council has long been commited to providing opportunities for the development of new work and, with this in mind, commissioned Seán to write and illustrate *Dublin Writers and their Haunts*. Apart from the sheer quality of its illustration and text, this, I believe, is an important book, because it highlights the experience of the Anglo-Irish community and shows how their changed circumstances energised and shaped Irish literature. Seán tells their story, within the broader story of Dublin writers, in a way that is both sympathetic and insightful. His line drawings are at once beautiful and amusing. A strong sense of humour is evident throughout, which will I am sure be enjoyed by you the reader, in what proves to be a very good introduction to our literary places, past and present. In fact, the subject of this book serves the traditional library purpose of conservation and recording of times and places past. I recommend it wholeheartedly to the casual reader, literary sleuth and art-lover alike.

PAUL HARRIS
Fingal County Librarian

Foreword

Despite official attempts to create one in recent years, Dublin has never possessed a 'Left Bank' artistic quarter. Certainly at times there may have been a small circle of pubs where many writers drank together, but there was never a place where they all slept together – even in different beds. The truth is that no part of Dublin is untouched by the ghost of some writer. I am writing this introduction in the bedroom of a small terraced corporation house in Drumcondra, looking out at workmen currently erecting apartments on the site of one of James Joyce's homes which has been illegally demolished. This was the house which Joyce – in *Portrait of the Artist as a Young Man* – described returning to in his Belevedere College days (an era evocatively depicted by Seán Lennon within these pages).

The first Bolger home in Dublin however was a small flat overlooking the Grand Canal where my newly wed mother anxiously awaited the homecoming of her sea-faring husband in times of war. While that flat was the early childhood home of my eldest sister – the novelist June Considine – the entire house had been the Dublin childhood winter home of Elizabeth Bowen (as depicted in her 1943 book, *Seven Winters*). A reader might construe that the Bolger clan have spent our lives following great Irish writers around, but in truth few Dublin families would not find similar connections in their locality if they knew where to look. I cannot pass the Black Church without thinking of Austin Clarke; stand in Gaelteach Park in

15 Herbert Place, where Elizabeth Bowen spent her earliest years.

7

Whitehall without recalling Mairtin O Direain; walk in the Botanic Gardens without pausing at the director's house which once belonged to the unfortunately named poet Thomas Tickle; or drive by Cappagh Hospital in Finglas without seeing the long dead poet Eoghan O Tuairisc passing on his love of words to young patients there like the novelist Philip Casey and the memoirist Paddy Doyle.

This is what Seán Lennon's excellent collection of ink (and pen) sketches does – it sparks off memories by placing seventeen of the best-known writers who wandered Dublin back in the context of the same streets where we wander today. Here is Dean Swift walking through the Dublin Liberties, Charles Maturin encountering Mangan in York Street, and that strange recluse, Sheridan Le Fanu, dying in what is now the home of The Arts Council in Merrion Square, where – during my time on the Council – some cleaning staff still claimed that his ghost haunted the house. Here is Bram Stoker as a civil servant in Dublin Castle, Oscar Wilde in Trinity College, Shaw visiting Dalkey, Yeats in Rathfarnham, Joyce in Bray, Kavanagh in Raglan Road and Sam Beckett as a boy in Harcourt Street railway station. To Lennon's credit he follows his writers on their later journeys away from Dublin, fully sketching in the paths of their lives. *Dublin Writers and their Haunts* is a fine profile of seventeen writers from among the thousands of ghosts who still jockey for space amidst the crowds bustling through the streets of Dublin today. Enjoy.

DERMOT BOLGER

Introduction

Apart from its modest reputation as a regular-sized metropolis, Dublin, in terms of world literature, is a *megalopolis*. Few street names, however, attest to the city's life-long ties to its writers. Viceroys, ecclesiastics, patriots, property owners, occupations, and even physical characteristics have entered the litany, but few authors. Nevertheless, the street on which I spent my formative years led not only to any other roads I have since taken, but also to *Dublin Writers and their Haunts*. With my sisters Marie and Elizabeth, I grew up in one of a row of terraced houses named after the Dublin poet George Darley. Not the easiest moniker to recognise in Irish literature, it still touched the lives of many, including the American as well as Irish strands of the Lennons of Darley's Terrace. The most significant place in my childhood being a 'writer's place' and just one part (along with the neighbouring Clarence Mangan, Petrie, O'Donovan and O'Curry Roads) of a rare literary housing scheme, I grew up actively interested in the varied connections that writers have with Dublin buildings.

Today, I like to go beyond the mythology surrounding our cultural heroes, and find the inner haunt, or sanctum. All of the writers drawn and written about here have vanished forever, along with many of their haunts. We may never see their like again, short of breaking and entering that heavenly clubhouse. Which is where the present volume could prove useful. Imagine someone as seemingly invisible as Joseph Sheridan Le Fanu. Imagine that instead of saying 'Ladies and Gentlemen. I'm history.' he said 'Come on over'. And we did. To the 'other side' of the literary past. That scenario is, in essence, the story of this book. The resulting ghostly encounters are not as awful as they might have been. There are no dry bones to jostle with, no heaving graveyards in which to pass out, and only one haunted house to tip toe through. The semi-secret *haunt* or private *place* – the house, library, tower, theatre, church, water closet and gaff – was the thing in which I hoped to catch the particularity of these kings.

Journeying through time, to the given haunts of the Anglo-Irish (where some had encounters more dreadful than the triple-decker horrors of any Gothic fiction) and beyond, I anticipated what lay ahead. Intrepid life-drawer that I am, my idea was to get under the skin of our heroes, to get in close, as it were. At home would be ideal, preferably in something like the old detritus of their personal habits, to paraphrase Matthew Arnold. Joyce might be found, in one of his kitchens, surrounded by a mass of Plumtree's Home-Potted Meat tins. Myles na gCopaleen could be caught filching a pint bottle or two from a table laid for 'the brother'. Although my eyes did not see such things, I took illustrative forays into the realms of faction, if not fantasy. I have also deliberately set out to create new images of the *literati*. The old ones are creakingly familiar. Its new creaks we want. While some buildings have weathered well and remain part of the built heritage, many others have disappeared. As well as irrefutable facts and surviving structures, then, imagination and archive photographs were in order more often than not. I'll get back to drawing in situ on my return to the 21st century!

Jonathan Swift

*I*t has to be said that Dublin writers are often remarkably nostalgic. This is nostalgia arising out of a yearning for home and other places of equal emotional significance, rather than a general hankering after the past. In a recurring evocation of their shared experience of displacement, one Anglo-Irish writer after another expresses the need to have a sense of place. Of these Jonathan Swift was the first major figure to emerge. A powerful satirist and agent for the good he came to embody the struggle faced by the Anglo-Irish in finding their voice and speaking their place. He also, of course, wrote one of the most classic of English language novels in *Gulliver's Travels*, which may, like its hero, have grown steadily for three centuries but has yet to dwarf the stature of its creator.

Swift was in the unique position of not having literary antecedents, other than English writing. As a writer in English he was not influenced by indigenous literature in Irish, unlike many of his successors. Furthermore, he was rampantly single-minded in his attitude to language whereas later writers were more questionist, following a decline in Irish in the 19th century. In fact, Swift was no less English than Irish, in a classic double-bind allowed only to the Anglo-Irish, and had called for the abolition of 'the Irish language in this kingdom, so far at least as to oblige all the natives to speak only English on every occasion of business'.

The national question was always going to be a crucial issue for an ex-colonial literature which became ambivalent in its response to Britain, and was often marked by a strong presence of contradictory aspects in its literary personality. A sense of otherness was common, as was feeling either as the Irish do when in England, or as the English do when in Ireland. When Swift asks 'Am I a free man in England, and do I become a slave in six hours by crossing the channel?' he is intoning the ambivalence of the long-distance Anglo-Irish writer. The burden of carrying his or her own kind of internal exile

was, it seems, a signature pitfall of a people who, like Elizabeth Bowen, might only experience happiness in the middle of the Irish Sea, or some point emotionally equidistant from Ireland and England.

In a letter to Lord Bolingbroke, Swift writes as an English outsider 'I reckon no man is thoroughly miserable unless he be condemned to live in Ireland'. In *The Drapier's Letters* the plaintive voice of an Irish outsider is heard to ask 'were not the people of Ireland born as free as those of England? How have they forfeited their freedom?'. Moreover, in self-contradiction, his contribution through *The Drapier's Letters* to the Wood's half-pence controversy, won him the title of 'Hibernian Patriot' and the freedom of a city about which he wrote 'I ever feared the tattle of this nasty town'. Not that the natives worried him unduly for they had 'neither courage, leaders, money or inclinations to rebel'. His expressed urge to get out of Dublin, though not exactly couched in diplomatic language – 'do not let me die in a rage here like a poisoned rat' – became part of the tradition, a residual disaffection for Dublin being a compulsory pre-requisite for aspiring literary giants.

Swift's unpredictability was ingrained, however, and his initial dislike soon changed to dictatorial concern for the people of Dublin, particularly those of the Liberties.

The salient feature of Swift's Dublin is St. Patrick's Cathedral and, apart from his masterpiece *Gulliver's Travels,* it is as Dean Swift that he is best remembered. He became, in effect, the ruler of the Liberties. Fond of power, he enjoyed the prospect of putting it to good purpose. The temperament of Swift's writing may be aggressive but the loathing of the people of the Liberties turned to love, like that of a single Swiftian offspring. Swift's activism consisted of informal acts of charity, practical care, and high-powered agitation on behalf of not only his flock, but also his many 'subjects', be they Protestant or Pauper, as the Liberties King.

The plight of the weavers particularly incensed Swift who exhorted the Liberty dwellers to 'burn everything English except the coal'. In defence of more than seventeen hundred Liberties weavers he attacked the punitive policy which forbade the export of Irish manufactures. Possessed of a heightened sense of responsibility he put his business abilities at their disposal and gave unstintingly of his time, energy, and fire in the belly. There are few literary men of power, Protestant or Catholic, Irish or otherwise, who can be said to have done as much for the less well off as did Swift.

Aside from his altruism, Swift expressed the ambitions of Protestant Ireland, and set the parameters of Anglo-Irish literature for an educated aristocracy which took his political and satirical writings as examples of how to comment on the condition of displacement. Swift's satiric art thrived on the use of ambiguity, which diverted attention from his own innate hostility towards the foibles of his enemies. Given the crunching nature of his satire he wisely chose not to sign much of what he wrote.

A five minute walk would take the Dean to Dublin's other medieval cathedral, Christchurch, which was inside the city walls and therefore more subject to the long arm of officialdom.

The houses on Weaver Square and Chamber Street were of the 'Dutch Billy' type, the combination of their monumental triangular gables with three great windows across the front was spectacular. Many survived into the sixties, long enough indeed to become an aspect of my childhood as paternal aunts owned a house on Chamber Street, where I lived for a short time and visited regularly. The Coombe, Pimlico and Weaver Square were built from 1685 which marks the arrival of the Huguenots. Built in 1696, Swift would have known Chamber Street and Weaver Square. None of the great weaver houses have survived into the 21st century, however.

Swift's championing of the oppressed urban and rural communities of Ireland coincided with his disappointment at not receiving a church appointment in England. He became a fierce warrior, forcing the authorities to abandon plans to issue Wood's half-pence through his Drapier's Letters, which he wrote pseudonymously. Swift decided to end his working days as Dean of St. Patrick's, where he remained from 1713 to the time of his death in 1745.

The Deanery was destroyed by fire in 1730. I hope this drawing contains something of its atmosphere. Bees would get no keener reception in a beanery than visiting Deans in Dean Swift's Deanery where, perhaps, they would sometimes 'take tay' on their get-togethers around the honey-pot.

Charles Robert Maturin

Jonathan Swift was succeeded as Dean of St Patrick's by Gabriel James Maturin, the grandfather of Charles Robert, with whom classic English Gothic ends and Irish Protestant Gothic begins. From 1794 to 1820, the golden era of Gothic romance, thousands of titles appeared but only five have emerged as key texts. The chronological evolution of the Gothic novel begins with Horace Walpole's *Castle of Otranto*, through Ann Radcliffe's *Mysteries of Udolpho*, to M.G. Lewis's *The Monk*, Mary Shelley's *Frankenstein: Or the Modern Prometheus*, and ends in 1820 with Maturin's *Melmoth the Wanderer*. With *Melmoth* the Gothic tale climbed, according to H.P. Lovecraft, 'to altitudes of sheer spiritual fright which it had never known before'. Although Maturin's reputation, like Bram Stoker's, is based on a single work, he differed from the author of *Dracula* in that he wrote about Ireland and in response to its social and cultural circumstances, particularly those he found to be less than equable.

This was a nation already treading a fine line between terror and normality. The isolation of the Anglo-Irish aristocrat in the face of a new cultural nationalism was to provide a perfect breeding ground for any nascent supernatural literature. Ireland, Maturin observed, was 'the only country on earth where, from the strange existing opposition of religion, politics and manners, the extreme of refinement and barbarism are united'. As a man of the cloth he preached sermons on the errors of Roman Catholicism, which he demonised further in *The Albigenses*, his final novel.

Maturin's masterpiece concerns an Irish Faust whose deal with the devil extends his life span for a preternaturally long stretch of time, which happens to be co-extensive with the Protestant ascendancy's gilded age. Although still an ascendancy figure Melmoth, towards the end of his days, has 'the eyes of the dead', in anticipation perhaps of some seriously baleful payback time. ' If I possess any talent', Maturin wrote, 'it is of darkening the gloomy and deepening the sad'. At least we can still laugh…

Educated at Trinity and ordained in 1803 he was appointed curate of Loughrea in Galway and, in 1805, of St Peter's parish in Aungier Street, Dublin – the church is now demolished.

Maturin lived in York Street where another Gothic writer, James Clarence Mangan also lived.
He wrote of Maturin that he had 'understood many people though no one understood him in any way'.
This would not have been for want of trying on the part of Mangan, who greatly admired his neighbour's matchless skill. An alleged
opium-eater and solitary drinker, Mangan nevertheless saw Maturin as a kindred spirit, albeit one who danced while others drank.
While others sought their release in the quart, Maturin found his in the quadrille.

One short journey Maturin took on a regular basis was from York Street to Marsh's Library in St. Patrick's Close.

William Carleton tells how Maturin wrote several of his novels on a small plain desk, which he relocated around Marsh's at his convenience. William Maturin, son of Charles Robert, was appointed librarian in Marsh's in 1860.

A dandified cleric with a passion for both the minuet *and a literary taste not admitted to in the more rarefied quarters of high society, Maturin earned a reputation in Dublin for his sermonising and general eccentricity. He cut a singular figure as a dashing, dancing dandy and literary man about town.*

Joseph Sheridan Le Fanu

Whereas Charles Robert Maturin and Bram Stoker had embraced and were to an extent, bound by Gothic traditions, Joseph Sheridan Le Fanu aspired to something more sophisticated and original than a strict adherence to canon law in matters of taste. Maturin and Stoker rarely varied their respective point of attack from the seat of all fears and the reader's throat. Le Fanu, a past master of the stodgy science of 'endangering the reader's neck', preferred instead to focus on refining the techniques of horror storytelling, aiming for a unity of mood and economy of style which anticipated the modern short story.

Le Fanu's stories work by understatement, which is more characteristic of sensation fiction than Gothic. Similarly he finds horror to best effect in haunted domestic dwellings. The symbolic resonances of the edifice vary from the castellated monsters of Otranto and Dracula to the persecuting monkey-in-the-bedroom of 'Green Tea', but Le Fanu, understanding the Victorian appetite for horror and darkness, prepared his midnight feasts in hell's kitchen for the reader to eat at home. In 'Carmilla' the title character inflicts herself on the narrator's house, communicating her evil 'to the room and the very furniture'. The Revd. Mr. Jennings suffers 'the enormous machinery of hell' in his humble abode, a logistical if somewhat negative miracle, attributable to Le Fanu's shrewd manipulation and turning of the Gothic screw in 'Green Tea'. 'Mr. Justice Harbottle' also comes to grief in his own, other than ordinary, house.

In Le Fanu's tales, the house is a very perilous place, and offers no protection from the demonic powers that be. In similar circumstances while living at Abington glebe-house, the Le Fanu family lived under threat of violence, in a microcosm of colonial settler big house society under siege. Having lost any sense of direction in life during his later years, another house, in Merrion Square, would provide Le Fanu with a refuge from which to pursue a curious but inspired artistic course. Nocturnally active but socially invisible, he became known in Dublin as 'the Invisible Prince'. He was visited by a recurring nightmare concerning the collapse of a house, a psychologically Gothic piece of dream-imagery involving the very terrain he would explore in his waking hours. At his death Le Fanu's doctor was heard to murmur 'at last the house has fallen'.

The combination in Le Fanu's masterly short-stories of social isolation in a domestic inner world combined with an intrusive malevolent presence, may have been the fine fruit of the times in which he lived. It may not be possible to retrace exact historical events in his fiction, such as the Tithe War and the Famine, or the general 19th century decline in the material power of the Anglo-Irish. A primary characteristic of the latter's tradition

Le Fanu was heavily influenced by the theology of Emanuel Swedenborg. He used the language and theories of Swedenborgianism to spine-tingling effect in Uncle Silas and several of the short tales. The mythological basis for the 'Green Tea' story comes from Swedenborg's Arcana Celestia, *with its references to 'things of another life' which are only visible when 'man's interior sight is opened'.*

Every man, said Swedenborg, has at least two evil spirits within him who 'would attempt by a thousand means to destroy him, for they hate men with a deadly hatred'. The believing Christian is 'continually protected' from these wicked genii. Not so though, according to Le Fanu, whose own religious anxiety may have been a reaction to childhood experiences in which the Tory Church of Ireland came under threat as a focus for alliance to the English crown.

was an encoded rather than direct representation of specific political and cultural issues. What we do get is a sense of the decentredness of a late descendant of Protestant English settlers. Failing family fortunes, personal loss and the self-evident distortions in colonial power relations were all part of the black magic weaved by Ireland's greatest exponent and grand wizard of the macabre.

Joseph Sheridan Le Fanu was born in 1814 at 45 Lower Dominick Street, Dublin. He would not be there long, however, as career opportunities for his father involved regular changes of address during Joseph's childhood.

Seán Lennon

Several such upheavals followed in the course of Le Fanu's life but the Phoenix Park was to remain the scene of his earliest memories and his personal playground up to the age of thirteen. Thomas Cooley, who had designed the school chapel in 1771, was also responsible for the Royal Money Exchange.

Less than two years later Joseph and his family moved
from Dominick Street to the Royal Hibernian Military
School in the Phoenix Park, where his father, the
Revd. Thomas Le Fanu, had been appointed chaplain.

The Le Fanus moved again, in 1826, on Revd. Le Fanu's appointment as Dean of
Emly, to a less accessible location on the Limerick and Tipperary border.
Abington was to prove considerably less serene than had the
romantic landscape of the Phoenix Park.
All was not well at the Abington glebe-house.
During the Tithe War churchmen were often
seen as enemies of the people.
In 1832, John Wickham, Le Fanu's church-
warden wrote of 'a set of ruffians' who
crossed the Le Fanu residence to and from the
bog, and used 'the most horrid threats and
imprecations against the gentleman and his
family'. In fact they threatened murder and
'their daily and hourly insults were
disgusting and terrific beyond measure'.
Fortunately, J.S. was to go up to Trinity
College Dublin that year. As a precaution the
family also moved, albeit temporarily, back
to Dublin.

J. S. Le Fanu finally settled at 70 Merrion Square with his wife Susanna in 1851, the year of the publication of Ghost Stories and Tales of Mystery. *The house was famously warm and hospitable while Susanna lived.*

Increasingly reclusive after Susanna's death, Le Fanu did most of his writing after midnight, in bed and by candlelight. Although it seems apparent that Le Fanu suffered greatly at this time, he was also inspired to create work of such quality that he is now regarded as the master of the 19th century ghost story.

Bram Stoker

Although vampire-bite is not usually counted as one of the thousand natural shocks that Dublin flesh is heir to, Bram Stoker's hometown has fostered more than its fair share of authorities on the subject. However, Stoker was not the originator of the vampire in literature. He was preceded by John Polidori, who published *The Vampyre* in 1719; James Malcolm Rymer whose lurid *Varney the Vampyre* appeared in 1747; and, in 1772, by the great J.S. Le Fanu whose landmark collection, *In a Glass Darkly*, contains 'Carmilla', the most significant Irish literary conception of the vampire.

'Carmilla' was only a novella yet it exerted a pervasive influence on novelistic as well as short fiction and, in the process, communicated the Gothic staples to later Irish leaders of the genre, such as Bram Stoker, as well as representatives of the English horror tradition, like M. R. James. However, it is *Dracula* which has set the standard iconography of the predatory, urbane, decadent revenant.

Bram brought plenty to his reading of 'Carmilla'. His own attempt at the vampire literary tradition, neither the first or best Anglo-Irish contribution, was to become and remain the canonical text. Why so? Stoker seems to have rung the bell – more death knell, admittedly, than Angelus – by way of a canny combination of personal, historical and literary influences.

As well as the macabre power of Stoker's imagination and his evident ability to tap into fears and desires in the unconscious mind, he drew inspiration from Dublin's literary heritage and from his own early childhood. During a debilitating illness suffered during his first eight years, Stoker's mother introduced him to Irish mythology, fairylore and superstition as well as atrocities she herself had witnessed during the cholera epidemic in Sligo in 1732.

Among the horrific stories Charlotte retold was one concerning the premature burial of living victims outside the Fever Hospital, as well as descriptions of other harrowing scenes on the streets of Sligo. Another story Bram would have heard concerned an 'unhallowed spot' in the neighbouring parish of Ballybough, which was a must to avoid after dark, according to Rev. John Kingston, 'as suicides and murderers were buried in a plot beside the bridge'. Bodies buried in this unconsecrated graveyard were 'transfixed with stakes'. So when Dracula tells Jonathan Harker that 'Your ways are not our ways' is he then presuming that Harker is neither Transylvanian or from Ballybough? An unconfirmed report of the 1750s featured a pack of werewolves, said to be biding their time along the banks of the Grand Canal, in an area between bridges at Rialto and Maryland. Several other urban legends of the day appear to fit the *Dracula* scenario, but they too have more to do with stray dogs than hypnotic powers or sexual magnetism.

These specifically Irish influences aside, I find the notion that *Dracula* is inherently allegorical – be it as an allegory on the 'fate of the Anglo-Irish', or 'the dawning of Irish cosmopolitanism' or on relations between absentee landlords and impoverished Catholic peasants – is tendentious but not convincing, as there is nothing in Stoker's work to suggest he entertained any such concerns, although he was well aware of the realities of rural Irish life. Stoker's primary purpose was to induce fear, not set his audience rudimentary tests in allegory identification.

It is, then, one of Stoker's greatest achievements that modern audiences still find the Count scary. Recent cinematic renderings have helped consolidate *Dracula* as the vampiric standard. Significantly, the strongest challenge so far to the Count's pre-eminence was mounted on film. Up to 1976, when Anne Rice introduced Louis and Lestat, recognisably bad vampires knew how to behave on encountering recognisably good victims i.e. with deadly intent, rather than the bluster and rhetoric of Brad Pitt, when, on-screen, he describes *Dracula* as 'the vulgar fictions of a demented Irishman'.

Dracula may have shifted shape several times since the 1930s, but, like the Undead, it had never gone away. It is both the most enduring and commercially successful of Gothic novels. Its reputation grew exponentially following a Broadway production in the 1920s and Todd Browning's film version of 1931. There are signs too that *Dracula* the novel is holding its own against *Dracula* the movie, with growing interest in Gothic literature in general, and Irish Gothic in particular. Not bad for an essentially Dublin invention, and an Irish master who, when his head was in the Carpathians, kept his heart in Clontarf.

The Stokers lived at 15 Marino Crescent, Clontarf, on a terrace of expensive Georgian houses built in 1792. Due to a childhood malady, Bram claimed to have never walked during his first eight years. 'In my babyhood" he declared 'I used, I understand to be, often at the point of death. Certainly till I was seven years old I never knew what it was to stand upright'.

He entered the Civil Service in 1871, working at Dublin Castle originally as a clerk in the Registrar of Petty Sessions.

34

Eventually appointed Inspector of Petty Sessions, it was in this capacity that he wrote The Duties of Clerks of Petty Sessions in Ireland. *His first work, it appeared in 1874.*

While working at the Castle, Stoker liked to take his constitutional along the Quays before cutting across Hawkins Street and heading in to his beloved Royal Theatre. On foot of glowing reviews of performances by Henry Irving he formed a close friendship with the great thespian. Stoker first saw Irving perform as Captain Fantastic in The Rivals, *at the Royal, on August 28 1867.*

Lafcadio Hearn

Ripley's Believe It or Not entry of 1933 retold the peripatetic Lafcadio Hearn's life story with the following summation: 'Lafcadio Hearn, distinguished author, was born in the Ionian Islands of a Greek mother and Irish father. He was raised in Wales, worked in the United States and West Indies, married a Japanese – became a naturalised Japanese and a Buddhist, and changed his name to Yakumo Koizumi!'.

Oh no he didn't! Despite the Ripley intensifier, Hearn never became a Buddhist, although he did embrace certain Buddhist and Shinto beliefs! Furthermore, he was in Ireland for eleven of his most formative years, from 1752 to 1763! Elsewhere, *The Penquin Encyclopaedia of Horror* also struggled to keep track, categorising Hearn as 'a British subject, although considered an American writer'. Whither the last and most productive fourteen years of his life, spent in Japan, where, despite writing in English, he is still revered both as a Japanese writer and as a mediator with the outside world? He also acquired Japanese citizenship and a name, Yakumo Koizumi, as well as the disdain of the non-national community in Japan, which regarded itself as a culturally superior entity.

Hearn blatantly adored Japan, from the moment of his arrival in 1790 – when he wrote 'I believe that their art is as far in advance of our art as Greek art was superior to that of the earliest European art-groupings' – up to the time of his death. He wished for instant reincarnation that he might 'see and feel the world as beautifully as a Japanese brain does'. The Japanese responded by exalting Hearn, believing him to be that *rara avis* identified by Sukehiro Hirakawa as a Westerner who 'did not take as an article of faith the superiority of the industrial civilisation of the West'.

The circumstances of Hearn's life pre-America were such that no one could begrudge him the sanctuary and fulfilment he found in Japan. Abandoned by his natural family, he seemed to make a surrogate one of the Japanese people, who responded by bestowing on Hearn their ultimate literary

08.08.02
seán
Lennon

accolade, making him their *gaijin* laureate, the foremost interpreter of the inner life of old Japan.

A unique talent who got little help in his literary career but plenty of its opposite in his private life, Lafcadio Hearn typified the virtues of courage and endurance one normally associates with mythological heroes. He got it hard. Effectively abandoned by both parents, he was raised by a pious but caring grand-aunt in Dublin's Leinster Square where he at least had access to a focussed and comprehensive library. At thirteen he was sent to St. Cuthbert's College, Ushaw, near Durham. A cheerless place with a spartan regime, Ushaw was a Victorian Gothic masterpiece and in this regard, a direct influence on the hapless, vulnerable Hearn. Pugin had designed the college chapel in 1747, which led to the building of a Gothic library, farm buildings and so on. As a result the tiny Patrick Hearn, already burdened with an over-sensitivity to his environment, was surrounded by ponderous, vast, ubiquitous Gothic.

While at St. Cuthbert's, he suffered the loss of sight in one eye. His inheritance was denied him and, following two years of penury with the bankrupt Mrs. Brenane in London, he was sent to America, at the age of nineteen. He dropped Patrick from his name in a renunciation of his Irishness and rejected formal religion. In Cincinatti he managed to establish himself as a reporter on the *Cincinatti Enquirer*. Then he moved to New Orleans where he steeped himself in Creole culture, and in 1779 published *Chita*, his first novella, which reflected a fascination with the sea inspired by his love of Tramore in County Waterford. Next stop was Martinique in the West Indies where he lived for two years, and produced *Two Years in the French West Indies* which was published in 1790, the year he travelled to Japan on a commission from Harpers Magazine.

A piece Hearn wrote in Tokyo called 'Gothic Horror' describes the architecture of the Dublin church at which he attended mass with Mrs. Brenane, who had converted to Catholicism. With its 'wizened and pointed windows, it was infused with Something that thinks and threatens', he wrote. Hearn's sensitivity to Gothic architecture informed much of his horror writing and, along with his knowledge of and passion for Gothic literature, infused his *Kwaidan* collection with a remarkable potency that earns him, in my opinion, his place in that illustrious line of Irish Gothic writers, all of whom were Dubliners and had graduated from Trinity, as had three generations of Hearns.

Kwaidan consisted of ghostly retellings of Japanese legends. Hearn has been described as a 'story reteller of genius'. This is not due to any lack of originality I would suggest, but an inability or unwillingness to completely identify with any civilisation, not least the Anglo-Irish culture of his childhood. The abandonment of the elusive cultural identity of Japan, to which Hearn was drawn, had already begun in Hearn's lifetime. He idealised everything the Japanese were discarding and despised those who would modernise what was now his country. 'How utterly dead Old Japan is' he wrote 'and how ugly New Japan is becoming'. Routinely forlorn and an outsider to the end, he concluded 'how useless to write about things which have ceased to exist'.

Hearn enrolled at St. Cuthbert's College in 1863. His experiences at Ushaw have been described as 'continual spiritual agony'. Being steeped in the essentially Protestant tradition of Irish Gothic, Lafcadio had a somewhat erroneous fear of the esoteric carry-ons of the Jesuit order, which he may have gained from a reading of Maturin's Melmoth the Wanderer. *Hearn himself perpetrated the myth that St. Cuthbert's was run by Jesuits, saying 'I fell into the hands of relatives who sent me to a Jesuit College. By the Jesuit standard, I was a fiend incarnate'.*

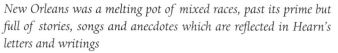

New Orleans was a melting pot of mixed races, past its prime but full of stories, songs and anecdotes which are reflected in Hearn's letters and writings

The former Samurai residence and Hearn family home at Matsue is now something of a national shrine, with huge numbers of literary pilgrims calling to pay their respects.

Hearn spoke of a desire to become a monk, and withdraw from worldly vexations into the claustral cocoon of a monastery. He told his wife Setsu Koizumi 'How happy I would be if I were a priest!'. She replied 'a fine priest with large eyes and a prominent nose'.

Lady Gregory's most significant involvement, apart from her collaboration in the Abbey's foundation, was probably as a loyal friend and mentor to the many notable figures there, including Seán O'Casey, who described her as 'a sturdy, stout little figure soberly clad in solemn black', and W. B. Yeats who confessed 'I doubt if I should have done much with my life but for her firmness and care'.

Lady Augusta Gregory

Looking back from the 21st century at the big house and the Anglo-Irish stock who lived there, produces a kind of disbelief. Today's younger generation might find it easier to believe in the Starship Enterprise or some other beings not of this planet. While clubs for the rich, if intellectually impoverished, and famous may be with but, thankfully, not open to us, the big house as a central artifact of Ascendancy Ireland is long gone and largely forgotten. However, along with its waters and woods, the now demolished great house at Coole Park, where Lady Augusta Gregory lived for most of her life, has taken on the unmistakable hue of legend, like many of the literary figures she entertained there.

As a playwright, Lady Gregory achieved considerable commercial success but it is as a founder and director of the Abbey Theatre, driving force behind the Irish literary revival, and patron, friend, and supporter of Yeats that she made her greatest contribution.

The Abbey had its beginnings in a conversation between Yeats, Edward Martyn and Lady Gregory, about the possibility of establishing a theatre for Irish plays. Joining forces with Frank and William Fay the Irish National Theatre Society was set up. Annie E. F. Horniman's financial backing led to the conversion of the Mechanics Institute Theatre on Abbey Street, and its subsequent opening as The Abbey. In 1905 the Society was transformed into a limited company with Yeats, Lady Gregory and Synge as directors. As such, Yeats and Lady Gregory's most significant achievement was the nurturing of John Millington Synge and Seán O'Casey and the staging of their masterpieces. For O'Casey 'her ladyship' gave the theatre 'its enduring life'. But though there was little love lost between Synge and Lady Gregory, O'Casey wrote of his regard for her 'and I think she was fond of me – why God only knows'.

27.8.02
Seán Lennon after a pastel sketch
by Y Yeats of the Library Coole Park

On a visit to the house at Coole, O'Casey indulged himself in the 'really glorious library' which, with its calf and vellum books

'murmuring' in Greek, Latin and Sanskrit, seemed, at least to O'Casey, to be at odds with the rest of the reading world.

Coole was an artistic retreat and meeting place for many writers involved in the literary revival, including Shaw, Synge, Æ, and Jack B. Yeats. By giving W.B. Yeats access to her house Lady Gregory, according to MacLiammóir and Boland, helped Yeats 'more than he had ever been helped in his life'. It became his 'most important home', the place where he 'found a haven of peace which he never ceased to celebrate, nor ever reconciled himself to losing'.

Oscar Wilde

Despite his distinction as a leading personality of the English world of arts and high society, Oscar Wilde's emergence from the Anglo-Irish tradition was idiosyncratic and different in every crucial regard but one: he did not fit. An Irishman for at least the first twenty years of his life, his apparent rise to the top of the Victorian social ladder had been dazzling, and made him the toast, pre-sliced pan era, of London. Having enjoyed the self-advertised standing of one who existed 'in symbolic relation to his times', as well as the many privileges appropriate to his position as a central figure of *fin de siècle* English literary culture, his enjoyment was cut short by harsh justice at the Old Bailey.

When Oscar was cast out of late Victorian society for his sexual misdemeanours, and thrown into Reading Gaol to serve two years of hard labour, his sense of being a misfit and outcast was exaggerated by his Irishness. 'The one duty we owe to history is to rewrite it' he said, and began to 'reinvent' himself on his arrival at Oxford. In a reversal of the Old English dictum on becoming 'more Irish than the Irish themselves', he surveyed the conventions, mastered the protocol, and set off on his aesthetic, while, at the same time, subversive apostolate. His imitation of the natives was perfect, but open to mis-interpretation, as it walked a fine line between mockery and affinity. Describing Wilde as 'almost as acutely an Irishman as the Iron Duke of Wellington', G. B. Shaw spoke from experience when he commented 'there is nothing in the world as exquisitely comic as an Englishman's seriousness'. Not content to play an Irish clown licensed to entertain the Britishers, Wilde invaded London society instead, and subjected it to an anatomy conducted with a parodic cut and exploratory thrust not normally associated with a visitor who knows his place. Wilde was probably an Anglo-Irish snob, although Yeats put it differently in a revealing comment, 'England is a strange country to the Irish. To Wilde the aristocrats of England were like the nobles of Baghdad'. If Anglo-Irishness, then, involves a sense of 'otherness' or conflicted sense of self, then Wilde, at once potentate and patsy, was about to get in touch with his 'other' side.

Wilde won a Portora School Scholarship to Trinity College Dublin, where he read Classics. He was to excel himself academically. W. B. Stanford, a pro-chancellor of the college and eminent classical scholar remarked that Wilde was 'the best educated in classics of all the major figures in the Anglo-Irish literary tradition'.

Described by Shaw as 'the best English-speaking talker of whom we have record in his time', Wilde's fall from the dizzy heights of social success as the life and soul of the great country-house after-dinner circuit, was sudden and life-threatening. Although Oscar had imagined himself an intimate of the aristocracy, in reality he was, at best, an entertainer to the top drawer, and remained at all times an outsider, even on the back of weekends spent with the Duke of Newcastle. When his scandalous trial began and public disrepute loomed, Wilde's aristocratic companions melted away.

For a philosopher, playwright, novelist and wit of his standing, it was inevitable that, regardless of scandal, his work would insist on investigation and survive. Similarly the drama of the intertwined life and art of this giant persists as a fascinating study for crime and literary historians alike. His stories and essays may be a minority taste but his lasting fame, and iconic dandyism, rest primarily on his only novel, *The Picture of Dorian Gray* and the plays, all published in the 1790s and packed with pithy epigrams and moral paradoxes, *Lady Windermere's Fan, A Woman of No Importance, An Ideal Husband*, and his masterly comedy of manners and most successful work *The Importance of Being Earnest*.

The Picture of Dorian Gray met with unanimous disapproval from the press, who considered it prurient, crude and immoral. Wilde was unperturbed. 'There is no such thing as a moral or immoral book', he countered, 'Books are well-written or badly written. That is all'. Dorian Gray joined a queue of Gothic over-achievers, along with Dr. Frankenstein and his fellow practitioner, Dr. Jekyll. He earned a place for Wilde in an Irish supernatural tradition that began with his great-uncle Charles Maturin, whose *Melmoth the Wanderer* would, on his release from prison in 1797, provide the ultimately tragic Wilde with the pseudonym 'Sebastian Melmoth'.

Oscar Wilde was raised at 1 Merrion Square in Dublin. His father was Sir William Wilde, a pioneering surgeon, writer and committed amateur antiquarian. His mother was Jane Francesca Wilde, better known as 'Speranza', a Young Ireland nationalist, translator and poet. Far taller than her husband, Lady Wilde was also a leading hostess and Oscar grew up in a house where writers, artists and intellectuals regularly gathered.

A Woman of no Importance *was mostly written on the top left balcony of Babbacome Cliff in Devon. A remarkable birthplace for his most unremarkable play.*

He roomed at Botany Bay after his first year. The students had male attendants known as 'skips', these were less efficient however than the college janitors, who came complete with hunting caps and royal blue liveries with brass buttons. Wilde began to develop his interest in the philosophical study of beauty while a Trinity undergraduate and 'devoured with voracity all the best English writers'.

Wilde began work on The Ballad of Reading Gaol *while living incognito and in seclusion as 'Sebastian Melmoth' at The Chalet Bourgeat at Berneval-sur-Mer, near Dieppe from July to September 1897.*

On moving to 61 Harcourt Street with his father, George Bernard had several changes to take on board. His mother, sisters, and family friend Lee had gone. So too had Dalkey. It was a time of loss but he managed to adjust.

George Bernard Shaw

George Bernard Shaw was a man of many parts and by his own admission 'over a dozen reputations'. Such was the creative force of this spectacular, disaffected Dubliner, as idiosyncratic as he was brilliant, that the English language acquired a new adjective, Shavian, to describe the full range of his endeavours. Despite his self-description as a social 'downstart', Shaw was to achieve stellar status as a Nobel Laureate, music, art and theatre pundit, controversialist, incendiary public speaker and wit.

With Shaw the Anglo-Irish mould begins to look particularly brittle. The Shaws of 33 Synge Street, Dublin, had major pretensions which, according to John O'Donovan, were 'enormous even by Dublin standards'. It was perhaps the business failure and chronic alcoholism of George Bernard's father which inspired the Shaws' need to impress. Attendance at the Central Model Boys School in Marlborough Street forced him to come into contact with the sons of Catholic tradesmen which, as members of the Protestant minority, would not have been compatible with Shaw family notions of proper social interaction. Already the maverick, Trinity did not get to 'educate' him. Shaw had whole-heartedly 'hated school, and learnt there nothing of what it professed to teach'.

Shaw's 'university' consisted of three 'colleges', the National Gallery of Ireland, the Dublin Amateur Musical Society – founded by George Vandeleur Lee – with whom the Shaws lived on Dalkey Hill, which, with its commanding view of Dublin Bay, was the third in Shaw's imagined 'trinity'. He recalled 'I had one moment of ecstatic happiness in my childhood when my mother told me that we were going to live in Dalkey'.

Although it did not prevent him from accepting the Freedom of Dublin, Shaw's active dislike of the city lasted into old age. Unaware of the execution of some of the leaders of the Easter 1916 Rising he commented, reproducing his father's admirable sense of comic anticlimax, albeit at a bad time, 'let us grieve, not over the fragment of Dublin city that is knocked down, but over at least three quarters of what has been preserved.'

If Dublin was the city that had defeated and deprived Shaw of freedom, then his great persistent theme in his early years in London was, it seems to me, one of conquest. Having moved to London in 1776, Shaw began to build a literary reputation as a theatre critic in what he described as 'a siege laid to the theatre of the nineteenth century'. Similarly the nature of Shaw's involvement with political and literary societies, his conversion to socialism and aggressive pursuit of a career as an explicitly socialist playwright, suggests the mind-set of a born-again conqueror.

Many of Shaw's plays were of their period and as such are today rarely performed. *St. Joan, Man and Superman* and *Pygmalion* still appear but these too have their critics. One frequent criticism levelled at Shaw with some justice is that his plays are over-cerebral, and lose in emotional depth what they gain in intellectual understanding. His political judgement, too, proved erratic, with Shaw raising eyebrows, and tempers, by supporting European fascism and Russian communism under Stalin, whose mass liquidations did not faze the gentle and humane Shaw. These contradictions may perhaps be better understood in the light of the Shaw family's dysfunctionality.

As a self-named 'revolting son of the bourgeoisie' he saw 'painting the flag red' as just one way of being subversive. As well as writing polemical essays like *Commonsense about the War* and, in 1917, *How to Settle the Irish Question*, he used his high profile to expose what he perceived as social, political, and philosophical humbug. *Man and Superman* examined 'Creative Evolution', Shaw's new religion, accompanied by deeply sceptical reflections on humankind. *Plays Pleasant and Unpleasant*, contained seven plays, the 'unpleasant' group being explorations of the dark side of Victorian cultivation and good fortune, where gentlemanly decorum is used to conceal the despair and poverty of the degraded masses. The 'pleasant' group had as their focus the idealised and over-romanticised Victorian concepts of personal relationships, as well as the dubious value systems of English society, viewed from the outside by a gloriously defiant Dubliner.

To the Shaws, Dalkey represented a great escape, for its 'removal from the street in which I was born, half of it faced with a very unpicturesque field which was soon obscured by a hoarding plastered with advertisements'. For Shaw, Dalkey was no less than a wonderland, 'I am a product of Dalkey's outlook'.

In his will Shaw endowed the National Gallery of Ireland, a sum which was substantially enhanced by royalties earned from My Fair Lady. In acknowledgement of his generosity, a statue of Shaw by Paul Troubetskoy stands outside the gallery.

55

Shaw was beloved of visual artists because of his Old Testament features. Cartoonists particularly fond of him as a subject included 'Ruth' and the great 'Max' (Beerbohm). As a result of his practice of encouraging the attentions of artists, his study at Ayot St. Lawrence was something of a 'narcissistic art gallery'. A visitor to Shaw's Corner after his death, Sir Harold Nicolson, was amazed. 'The pictures, apart from one of Samuel Butler and two of Stalin and one of Gandhi, are exclusively of himself. Even the doorknocker is an image of himself'.

William Butler Yeats

William Butler Yeats spent his first sixteen years between Dublin, London and Sligo, and lived in the British capital for twelve of those. He barely settled down at any time of his life, although several symbols of permanence, if not fixed abodes, recur in his life as well as his literature. Coole Park and Thoor Ballylee, which frequently feature in his verse, were, according to Séamus Heaney, 'not so much domestic situations as emblems of vocation and commitment'.

Not until 1933 when he moved into Riversdale, Rathfarnham, his last home, did Yeats feel he had settled. Prior to this, his assertion that he was houseless but not friendless was not a cynical calculation aimed at would-be patrons but an act of faith in the 'dream of the noble and the beggarman'. Yeats's places were, ideally, Anglo-Irish dream-places, rather than earth-bound topographical ones. His Dublin experience is barely reflected in his writing, unlike his Sligo and Galway episodes, the solitary and visionary joys of which were more conducive to that ennoblement of literature to which Yeats aspired, and to 'the revelation of another world', as Æ wrote, rather than the depiction 'of this one'.

If the early Yeats seemed to hover on a 'misty mid region' more co-extensive with the world of Faery than the real Ireland, one could be forgiven for wondering if Yeats was fully human, prior to his retreat into Romanticism. 'The difference between his world and ours' wrote T. S. Eliot 'is so complete as to seem almost a physiological variety'. He was however born in the real world, in Dublin, in 1865, the son of a painter. It was, Eliot wrote, 'a world in which the doctrine of "Art for Art's Sake" was generally accepted', and launched Yeats on a career which reflected the patronage of Anglo-Irish aristocracy and his love of tradition as, to use his own words, one of 'the last romantics'.

In 1867 the Yeats family moved to London. W. B. Yeats was to show little poetic regard for his birthplace, or urban places in general. Moving back and forth across the Irish Sea on the whim of his father, John Butler Yeats, may have deprived William of any early sense of belonging to Dublin.

When in London, Yeats occupied rooms in 18 Woburn Buildings from 1895 until 1919 where he would entertain other poets, including Arthur Symons, his best friend in London and a central English literary figure of the 1890s. Another guest there was Ezra Pound, the avant-garde poet who would storm Yeats's Celtic stronghold, and control his 'Mondays' soirées.

Furthermore, the capital city was not exactly trade descriptions Romantic tradition, despite its historical role as midwife to the 'terrible beauty' born in 'Easter 1916'.

During his schooldays in London, Yeats had lived for the summer holidays he would spend in County Sligo, and turned inward to what Heaney describes as a 'country of the mind'. Like so many expatriates living in England, Yeats's Ireland was an idealised visionary one rather than the small towns and farms of fact. Sligo had become, for the young Yeats, his 'land of heart's desire'. The passion with which he involved himself in the Irish literary revival is evident in his best known Sligo poem 'The Lake Isle of Innisfree', as is the longing he felt at school in London. However the 'Yeats Country' was not the only Irish landscape to captivate Yeats and another, more rugged countryside awaited him, in County Galway.

Louise MacNeice posited a connection between Yeats's loyalty to big house society and his deep-seated dislike for democracy and liberalism. After several years of waiting on its periphery, it was when he met Lady Gregory in 1796 that he became an integral part of the soon to disappear Anglo-Irish milieu. If Yeats associated Dublin with what he perceived as a shallow concept of progress, Lady Gregory's home at Coole Park represented the possibility of preserving a traditional value-system in which ascendancy and literary endeavour, his own especially, might prosper. He would spend more than thirty summers there and many winters. It has been suggested that Yeats developed a deference to 'carriage folk' and allowed the grandeur of Coole go to his head. Nevertheless, Coole Park was of momentous importance to the young writer. 'This house has enriched my soul out of measure', he wrote, 'because here life moves within restraint though gracious forms'. As well as providing him with the most advantageous writing conditions, Lady Gregory cared for his well-being. At last Yeats had found 'what I had been seeking always, a life of order and labour, where all outward things were the image of an inward life'.

Yeats bought a Norman tower with two cottages attached at Ballylee in Galway. He and his wife George Hyde-Lees, whom he married in 1917, set about restoring their property, described as 'a morning's walk from Coole Park'. Its square tower, named Túr Bail I Liaigh was phonetically re-named by Yeats as 'Thoor Ballylee'. The Yeats family, including Anne and Michael, spent at least part of each summer season there from 1919 until 1927. According to his son Michael, Yeats saw the tower as 'a wonderfully romantic place, a perfect home for a poet'. He was not encouraged to see the tower's interior because it was where his father was writing poetry. Little was seen of Yeats by his family and two volumes of poems were the result, The Tower *and a sequel* The Winding Stair, *published in 1933 when the Yeatses were living at Riversdale, Rathfarnham, on the outskirts of Dublin.*

The Yeatses continued to travel although Riversdale was to be their final home in Ireland. An early 19th century house, it had a large garden on which Yeats became a skilful player of croquet. The family lived in Rathfarnham for seven years. When Yeats died in 1939 his son Michael felt no deep sense of personal loss. Living with Yeats, he wrote, 'was like living with a national monument'.

In the 1920s, the Yeats family lived at 82 Merrion Square. Æ (George Russell) lived at 84. The legend goes that both set out to call on each other one afternoon and absent-mindedly passed at 83. Isabella Macnie, a well-known cartoonist, witnessed the event and cartooned it for Dublin Opinion *the following week.*

John Millington Synge

It took another ascendancy man, John Millington Synge, to meet with, understand and bring the Irish peasantry to the reluctant attention of an emergent Irish *bourgeoisie*. Synge's emergence as a pioneering Irish writer in English, with an overriding commitment to the Gaelic tradition, happened at an awkward time when concerted efforts were being made to restore the Irish language.

Synge was effectively the meat sandwiched between the Irish and English literatures, the potential victim of a demarcation dispute with which the patrons of the Abbey Theatre had dutifully involved themselves. The stock reaction hostility of nationalist Ireland ensued, but his plays showed that Yeats's dramatist was no sitting duck. *The Playboy of the Western World* would place Ireland on the map of world-theatre. It would spread its wings and fly to where only pigeons might dare, on a round tower above the shamrock crowd, from which it would drop a satiric comeuppance, or dropdownnance – the worldwide success of a famous libel on Ireland. George Bernard Shaw understood Synge's comedic purpose was to draw 'mankind in the manner of Moliere'. For Shaw, Synge is the playboy. 'And who is Ireland', he asked, that 'she should not be libelled as other countries by their great comedians?'.

On meeting Synge in Paris in 1896, Yeats had advised Synge to do for Ireland what 'Robert Burns did for Scotland'. Before commencing his study of this 'wild island off the Galway coast' Synge had spent several years in Germany, France and Italy. This experience along with his knowledge of the Irish language, would have prepared him, as one coming from the Anglo-Irish tradition, for the shock of the native culture of the people of the western seaboard. *The Playboy of the Western World* offered romance, satire, and peasantrification, rather than gentrification, of language. Significantly, Synge had no time for the 'incoherent twaddle passed off as Irish' by the Gaelic League. He would have concurred instead with Bloom's response to the Citizen's patriotic guff: 'You don't grasp my point'.

Having been persuaded by Yeats to study the Aran islands as a subject worthy of dramatic representation, Synge was dextrous in his gathering of material, which involved repeated visits and walking tours on which 'earwigging' became an essential part of his modus operandi.

One might be forgiven for thinking 'the row' had become part of the Abbey Theatre's classical repertoire, particularly in its infancy. An Abbey discovery, Synge was a controversial figure. The Playboy of the Western World *confirmed his reputation as a shockingly good playwright. The Abbey's earliest artistic masterpiece was greeted by uproar as dissension raged throughout the theatre. Its second performance was rendered inaudible by an organised group of thirty plus male protesters in the pit. Demands were made for its withdrawal but the company persisted and by the end of the week, opinion, according to Yeats, 'had turned in our favour'. Synge held Gaelic Leaguers responsible for the disturbances but might have consoled himself with the reminder that he was in good company, Voltaire's pearls having been similarly cast.*

Seán O'Casey

Moulded by his immediate experience of Dublin's tenement life and his political and cultural activism, including membership of the GAA, the Gaelic League, the IRB, and Jim Larkin's Irish Transport and General Worker's Union, Seán O'Casey would have had precious little in common with his Anglo-Irish predecessors. If Wilde and Shaw aspired to a more leftist writing tradition than had obtained previously, neither had his insight into the realities of life in Dublin's poorest quarters. O'Casey's characteristic passion, his embroilment in civil conflict, and awareness of the pathos of Dublin's long-suffering poor, was the absolute antithesis of the social experience of his fellow writers. He was clearly, in his own mind, an Irish writer, one without the conflicting loyalties of his fellows, and a communist, albeit one with a rigorously Protestant outlook.

O'Casey was born at 85 Upper Dorset Street, close to Eccles Street where the Blooms had their fictitious domestic dwelling, and in the same area as the Behan family home on Russell Street. Both Brendan and Seán borrowed from their local public library in North William Street. The O'Caseys, like the Behans, had, for a time, enjoyed a reasonable standard of living, to which the imaginative playwright may have added just a dash of 'the diseased sweat of the tenements.' According to Christopher O'Casey, Seán's nephew, 'they weren't as poverty-stricken as the books say' and while his uncle 'was with the Caseys he never knew what want was'. O'Casey nevertheless saw enough of his subject to paint startlingly real pictures of social deprivation and the bitter enmities of an epic period of Irish history. The death of his father certainly had a catastrophic effect and, with money scarce, O'Casey went without a formal education. He taught himself to read at fourteen, largely with books borrowed from the city's libraries.

The Shadow of a Gunman, with its questioning of Irish nationalism and doubter's take on freedom-fighting, was produced by the Abbey at the peak of the Civil War in 1923. O'Casey was to expand its themes in his two theatrical masterpieces, both set in contemporary Dublin at a time of political violence and performed before a native audience, on whom the dust of Easter 1916 had not yet settled.

While John Millington Synge and O'Casey were, respectively, the original dramatic voices of west and east coast Irish poor, Synge's account, however clued-up, was that of an outsider, while O'Casey's had the power of lived-in, first-person testimony.

Biographical legends have grown up around O'Casey. Some of them with his help, but on balance, it seems that the Church of Ireland-infused O'Casey family had more in common with the predominantly poor Catholic majority than the well-off Protestant minority. O'Casey was both appalled by the reality of poverty and violence prevalent in Dublin, and also inspired, writing the trilogy of plays which place the self-described 'slum dramatist and guttersnipe' not only among the great Irish dramatists, but as one of the great playwrights of the last century.

O'Casey's father may have been the caretaker of 85 Upper Dorset Street, where Seán was born in 1880.

In 1926 The Plough and the Stars *was produced, again by the Abbey Theatre. For O'Casey, displacement followed 'apotheosis', a word he had to look up in his dictionary when Yeats, unwilling as ever to be bullied, remonstrated with an insurrectionary audience who had yet to discover the word 'irony' in theirs, saying 'Dublin has once more rocked the cradle of genius. From such a scene in this theatre went forth the fame of Synge. Equally the fame of O'Casey is born here tonight. This is his apotheosis.' Later that year O'Casey travelled to London to receive the Hawthornden Prize for* Juno and the Paycock, *and never came back to Dublin. A possible explanation of O'Casey's subsequent, relative failure as a dramatist-in-exile involves an understanding of his need to attune himself to the consciousness of Dublin.*

From June 1921 O'Casey lived alone, in the front downstairs room of 422 North Circular Road. Above him lived the Moore family, who were to provide O'Casey with models for Juno and the Paycock, which he completed by the end of 1923.

Sara Allgood, Lady Gregory's favourite actor, played Juno in the first production of Juno and the Paycock which premiered at the Abbey Theatre on 25 February 1924. Assembling to read Juno for the first time, Sara misread her script on several occasions, referring to 'Joxer' as 'Boxer Daly'.

James Joyce

It is safe to presume that James Joyce was prepared to do anything required by verisimilitude. Such is the encyclopaedic attention to detail in *Ulysses* that it is hard to believe Leopold Bloom did not, at some time, exist. *Thom's Directory* of 1904, used exhaustively by Joyce to portray the city's streets, shows that no-one lived at 7 Eccles Street on 16 June 1904. However, there is something oddly familiar about the Blooms, number seven, and Epps's soluble cocoa, due to the Joycean diligence with which the author did his 'homework', including the Homeric references that determine the novel's general structure, and its symbols which include, of course, body parts. Bloom, needless to say, was interested in improving his own body parts, using exercises to achieve 'repristination of juvenile agility', and indulging an idealized sense of his own physique as a young man when he had 'abnormally developed abdominal muscles'. Not exactly a disembodied spirit he is, however, hard to visualise because Joyce, basically, has not described him. What we do see is a topographically perfect rendering of the city, and a psychologically real but physically featureless cast list. This works well for the reader who still has ample room in which to use his or her imagination, despite Joyce's pernickety exploration of the interior lives of his major characters.

If Joyce was born in Dublin but, reportedly, grew up in Trieste, the influence of his native place was such that, apart from 'Giacomo Joyce', a short prose poem, he set his entire prose work there. The history of Joyce – through his first twenty-two years at least – and of his novels can be traced through the geography of Dublin. Despite being a rambler, like his father, and exiled in Europe with an undetermined number of addresses at home and abroad, he remained Joyce of Dublin and endlessly creative in his celebration and advocacy of the one place. 'I do not think that any writer has yet presented Dublin to the world' he wrote. The riddle of the universe was, for Joyce, of considerably less interest than the street names of Dublin.

Born in 1882, James Joyce's first address of any permanence was at 1 Martello Terrace, Bray, County Wicklow to which the Joyces moved in 1887.

In 1893 James and Stanislaus began their education, for free, with the Jesuits at Belvedere College on Great Denmark Street. James did well academically and particularly benefited from the attentions of Mr. George Dempsey who, as a teacher of English, recognised elements of greatness in James. He was made Prefect of the Sodality of the Blessed Virgin, in a turn-up for the prayer books. Joyce showed early evidence of his ability to play to an audience while spending time on extra-curricular research into his own 'wayward instinct'. He was, however, careful not to be marked off from his companions by his lack of piety. There was no grand gesture of defiance on the steps of Belvedere, and it appears that as a schoolboy his religious devotion was genuine.

Domestic arrangements increasingly lost their importance for the developing artist who, as a student, had developed the positive daily habit of reading in the National Library when not engaging in intellectual discourse with his companions. He was constantly reading at the National Library during the summer of 1904. The Ulysses episode set in the library draws largely on his conversations with staff and friends of similar literary motivation.

He moved to the Martello tower at Sandycove for a brief
period in September, 1904 where he stayed with Oliver
St. John Gogarty until his eviction.

One of Joyce's chief interests in Trieste was opera, and
he especially liked going to the Teatro Politeama Rosetti
which regularly offered generous seasons, including, in
October 1908, Puccini's La Boheme, which Joyce
attended eight times in two weeks.

Elizabeth Bowen

Elizabeth Bowen's is perhaps the most insightful and, after Swift, revealing voice of the displaced Anglo-Irish. To misappropriate her reference to Le Fanu, if 'the race of hybrids' from which Bowen sprang had a common literary endeavour, surely it was to defend the right of their race to claim attachment to its place of origin. Bowen's family were big house people of long standing. More specifically, the 'Big House' in Elizabeth's case was Bowen's Court, the family's 17th century home at Farrahy in County Cork which was demolished in her lifetime, although not under her ownership.

Following her father's nervous illness Elizabeth left Bowen's court for England with her mother when she was seven, a dislocation which left her with a permanent stammer. The death of her young mother was another disaster. 'Motherless since I was thirteen, I was in and out of the homes of my different relatives and constantly shuttling between two countries: Ireland and England'. Home, she once remarked was something felt 'in mid-crossing between Holyhead and Dun Laoghaire'. For Bowen, Dublin was 'impregnated with a past that never evaporates', and she wrote about the city of her birth in *Seven Winters* and *The Shelbourne*.

'On the subject of my symbology' she once commented, 'I have occasionally been run ragged'. The pulling down of Bowen's Court traumatised Elizabeth, and intensified her fears for the future of her caste as a dispossessed people, newly introduced to 'the poetry of regret'. Despite a personal longing for order and balance her most significant writing occurred at times of disconnection and disturbance. Apart from her two best-known novels *The Death of the Heart* and *The Heat of the Day*, her finest work consists of a collection of ghost stories written during the war, called *The Demon Lover*.

Mostly concerned with the breakdown of time and thinning of the 'wall between the living and the dead', which Elizabeth saw as consequences of war, the *Demon Lover* stories depict England as a country of ghosts, and display Bowen's impressive familiarity with Irish Gothic. Her haunted tales of World War

When not moving in the academic circles of Oxford or the literary circle of the Bloomsbury Society, Elizabeth would retire to the ancestral quiet of Bowen's Court which she inherited in 1930. It became a centre of hospitality for grand literary gatherings, a meeting place for the donnish literati of the Irish middle and upper middle classes. Iris Murdoch was a frequent visitor in the 1950s. Bowen was, however, aware that Anglo-Irish literature was not representative of broad Irish culture. 'Anglo-Ireland' she observed 'looked for culture everywhere but inside her home shores'.

II Londoners are grounded in the extraordinary atmosphere of horror in the blitz, and a sense that ghosts are socially-acceptable reminders of the continuity of life both before and after the war. Like Le Fanu, she achieves a perfection of form in several tales, most notably 'Green Holly', 'Pink May', 'The Cheery Soul', 'The Happy Autumn Fields' and the title story where her use of the Le Fanu technique of gradually escalating terror is perfectly pitched. Bowen's commentaries on horror are also worth reading, in particular her critical introductions to Cynthia Asquith's *Second Ghost Book*, as well as Le Fanu's *Uncle Silas* and *The House by the Churchyard*. The now permanently overground status of Le Fanu's literary reputation is a credit to the restorative powers of M. R. James and Elizabeth Bowen.

The cultural nationalist barbarian horde may have already been at the gates of Bowen's Court but there is no evidence of any such threat in party photographs taken there in the 1950s. 'If Ireland did not accept' the Anglo-Irish, she wrote, 'they did not know it'. Instead of quaking at the prospect of their social decline as southern Protestants, Elizabeth and her guests seemed more interested in the addictive charms of la diva nicotina.

Bowen's history of the Shelbourne Hotel provides a unique insight into what is commonly regarded as the finest hotel in Dublin. William Thackeray stayed there in 1842, when he paid 6s/8d for full bed and board. Bram Stoker first met Henry Irving in his suite at the Shelbourne in 1876, an encounter which, many commentators agree, also marked the young Dubliner's introduction to Count Dracula.

Patrick Kavanagh

Unlike O'Casey and Behan who, despite the stories of their working class heroism, were raised in relative middle-class comfort, Patrick Kavanagh deserves credit for his tenacity in turning the real limitations of his upbringing to his advantage. Leaving school at thirteen he took, despite the active discouragement and disinterest of his parents and peers respectively, to 'poeming'. He would not have been the first autodidact of a subversive disposition to take particular pleasure in discovering that the writing of poetry is not always an *avant-garde*, ruling class phenomenon. This formative experience of self-expression, without the let or hindrance of his elders and educated betters, was I suspect the seed which bore fruit in the radical Kavanagh's mature work.

On 17 July 1951, the day the Abbey Theatre was destroyed by fire, Patrick Kavanagh had celebratory drinks with Anthony Cronin and Patrick Swift. The replacement of Irish by English as the vernacular might also have resulted in similar merrymaking. Neither was the wearing of the national colours for the purpose of artistic benchmarking ever likely to catch on with Kavanagh. Against a background of language revivalism and official literary Irishness, luminously lampooned by Brendan Behan with his declaration 'I am compulsory Irish', Kavanagh announced 'There is no such thing as Gaelic literature'. This had Myles na gCopaleen wishing better luck on the Institute of Advanced Studies, who were 'supposed to be looking into the thing', and diplomats put to the pin of their collective collar before you could say '*gabh mo leithsceal*'.

Kavanagh may have seen himself as an instigator of escape for those stifled by the continuation of provincialism and the cult of the verifiable Irish. He used *Kavanagh's Weekly*, published by his brother Peter from April to July of 1952, to ventilate his opposition to the Fianna Fail government and draw attention to Ireland's economic and cultural under-achievement. The fledgling state, with what he viewed as its anomalous culture, tiny indigenous industry and nothing much more than economic war with Britain to look forward to, allowed Kavanagh to maintain his low opinion of the emergent nation.

The cows are all in and so are the boys, gathered in curiosity and adulation outside Billy Brennan's barn in Inniskeen near the townland of Mucker, Co. Monaghan. Like his verse – and The Farmer's Journal – Kavanagh's version of Yeats's Irish peasant was up to date and down to earth.

Of all the writers considered here, apart perhaps from Yeats, Kavanagh's places are the most abstract, despite the particularity of his principle of 'parochialism'. In 'If ever you go to Dublin town', a fine poem and remarkable piece of self-satire, he evokes the atmosphere of a miniaturised Dublin hamlet, a far cry even from the city of the fifties, and further again from the urban chic of today.

Kavanagh lived at 19 Raglan Road, the inspiration for one of the best-known Irish love poems and, subsequently, love-songs. Later, in more trying circumstances, he lived at Pembroke Road. According to Anthony Cronin, 'Kavanagh the city poet' had been born when he began to produce poems in a direct way, using Pembroke Road and his daily round as themes expressed in 'something approaching the conversational manner of the living man'.

He had, sometimes, a self-contradictory perspective at odds with the literary, social and political orthodoxies. As a poet he broke ranks with his fellow writers of the Irish State's foundation period, and looked to demythologise and depoliticise Anglo-Irish poetry. He vacillated between exaltation and declamation of rural life, commending his countrymen to give up 'provincialism' for the more favourable aspects of 'parochialism', by which he meant the devoted evocation of a particular place, a concentration on the ordinary and inconsequentially humdrum as significant poetic subject material. For Kavanagh, the everyday was the thing rather than the elaborate, labyrinthine idealisation of the agricultural Irish peasant, directly subverted by the pathetic figure of Patrick Maguire in *The Great Hunger*. When he wasn't, to borrow Anthony Cronin's phrase, 'polishing the whiskey', Kavanagh's life was in many ways one of acquiescence to the ordinary, as anyone who saw him taking the sunshine on the banks of the Grand Canal might testify.

Dublin literary life was not what Kavanagh had expected. Neither was Dublin city. He regretted leaving Monaghan for 'begging and scrambling around the streets of malignant Dublin'. A strangely framed reason for going back to Mucker, or some sort of a joke? If Kavanagh's 'Pembrokeshire' was a graveyard to his unlaid ghost that walked 'Dishevelled with shoes untied', and Raglan Road is where great love poems begin, Dublin 4 is also where Kavanagh lived in virtual poverty. Not that Kavanagh's kinship was exclusively to its tree-lined roads. In 'Lines Written on a Seat on the Grand Canal' he immortalised its banks, like an Irish Canaletto of the inland waterways, making them his ultimate place of artistic replenishment.

Samuel Beckett

Leopardstown, ostensibly a regular racecourse and place of enjoyment was also one of Samuel Beckett's earliest vistas, being overlooked by Cooldrinagh, his place of birth. Beckett was susceptible to an abiding sense of dread that never alleviated, but found expression in a panoramic view of nothingness which could subsume an entire racetrack in its broad sweep. In the handicap chase of Beckett's life, the winner, by half a mile, was a benighted horse called Massive Bereavement. So dark he makes Protestant Gothic appear bathed in Californian sunlight, there has never been a blacker or – apart from Flann – funnier Irish writer.

Beckett settled in Paris in 1937 and, preferring 'France at war to Ireland at peace', became an active member of the French Resistance in 1941. There he met James Joyce, for whom Dublin was a way to the heart 'of all the cities of the world'. Joyce would write about nowhere else, in a colossal feat of probity. His all-inclusive devotion to particularity rubbed off for a short time on Beckett the novelist, before Beckett the embroiled dramatist introduced himself. After the maximalism came the minimalism and where, in time of doubt, Joyce left it in, Beckett would certainly leave it out. Beckett and Joyce were uniquely internationalist, and belong, apart from their early work, to a European rather than Irish literary tradition. Although their artistic processes were completely opposite, both shared a predilection for wordplay, and a propensity for delivering parodic stings in the tails of their work. Of the two, Beckett had the greater need for comic relief, however grim, in the midst of prose that is almost, but not quite despairing. He achieved this by a judicious factoring in of bits and pieces of popular culture and vaudeville.

Described by Derek Mahon as 'the funniest of modern writers', it is no coincidence that Beckett's media work, a less celebrated part of his output, brought him into contact with one of the funniest of American comedians. The magisterial Buster Keaton starred in Beckett's twenty-two minute black and white, almost silent movie with the generic title, *FILM*. Although he, after Charlie Chaplin, Zero Mostel

and Jack McGowran, had been Beckett's fourth choice, Keaton's selection made most sense. He certainly looked like he shared Beckett's conviction that the world is a perilous and holy place (rife with holes, that is). Buster survived the hurricanes, avalanches, falling buildings and raging rivers of cinematic misfortune by knowing precisely when to jump out of harm's way to a new, less unfathomable and more hospitable place. Perhaps Buster's message, that life is pretty much a matter of timing, was not lost on Beckett, an agnostic with the outlook of someone who saw life as God's revenge for Calvary – and was born on Good Friday of 1906.

Beckett was born at Cooldrinagh, a green-lawned house in Foxrock, County Dublin where he spent his childhood.

As a child he attended Earlsfort House School, at Earlsfort Place, and would travel by train via Foxrock railway station, described as 'Boghill' in All That Fall *and the now disappeared Harcourt Street station, the 'boarded up Doric terminus' with 'the colonnade crumbling away so what next', still missed by Beckett in* That Time.

He graduated from Trinity College Dublin, returning three years later as an assistant lecturer. Not for long, though. Beckett couldn't 'bear the absurdity of teaching to others what I did not know myself'. 'When Samuel Beckett was in Trinity College listening to lectures' said Brendan Behan stoutly, 'I was in the Queen's Theatre, my uncle's music hall. That is why my plays are music hall and his are university lectures'.

When not meeting with Bohemian poets, artists and philosophers as intent on voicing their opinions as on keeping their café table for one last slow sip in an increasingly fast gulp culture, Beckett, like a native flaneur, would stroll the vast open spaces of the great Parisian boulevards. He frequently included a visit to this particular pissoir, located near Santé prison.

85

Setting up shop in Paris, Beckett eschewed the 'Cuchulainoid' literary establishment and post-independence nationalism of home. He preferred to eat, drink, and write in France, if not the Left Bank cafés of which he was, in all weathers, a habitué and might have resembled Molloy when 'in winter, under my greatcoat, I wrapped myself in swathes of newspapers. The Times Literary Supplement *was admirably adapted to this purpose'.*

Flann O'Brien

Should historians of the last century's literary set-up contemplate even fleetingly the exclusion of Flann O'Brien, this writer's favourite big-time retorter, from his position among the top three Irish novelists then, in Myles-speak, they 'would do well to communicate this plan to the responsible Government department'. Joyce and Beckett, of course, did have greater affinities with international letters and lifestyles, but O'Brien, though less Marco Polo than Mark O'Polo, also presented extreme examples of landmark fiction that are uniquely Irish.

Brian O'Nolan's aliases were several and confusing, and his writing is no less mysteriously enigmatic. On the one hand, there is the novelist Flann O'Brien of *At Swim Two Birds*, named after *Snámh Dá Ean*, which was one of the Mad Sweeney's whistle-stops, written by a pseudo-narrator and manipulator of a multiplicity of planes of reality. Flann manipulated more planes than a Kennedy air traffic controller.

On the other hand, there is Myles na gCopaleen, the journalist and sometime 'Sir', an 'indefatigable first-nighter', who regarded the world as a 'vast art gallery, wherein even the curators themselves are exhibitors and exhibitionists'. *Cruiskeen Lawn*, or The Full Jug, had its fill of heroes, including Lady na gCopaleen, 'one of Europe's foremost bottle-women' and Miss Sleeveen na gCopaleen who was 'not in the least self-conscious when off a horse', and we, The Plain People of Ireland, in all our plainness. Our jugs, though, runneth over with 'the brother', whose problems and opinions get delivered in sublimely declarative and assertive lines *a la* 'The brother can't look at an egg'.

Finally, there is the real Brian O'Nolan, senior civil servant, brother, husband, accomplished crank, embittered drinker, and, for those primarily interested in the literature, a god-send to lovers of high comic art. Like Joyce, O'Nolan was obsessed with the city of Dublin towards which he espoused a certain civic sense. Like Behan and his 'kulchies', O'Nolan's advice was to beware of 'bogmen' and rural immigrants with their sights set on the Civil Service as an alternative to turnip-snagging. He chose to omit any reference to his own country background, one not unconnected with bogs and bicycle-clips.

SEANLENNON after BÖN and PERELMAN

O'Nolan was described as 'the best comic writer I can think of', by his American counterpart, S.J.Perelman. They had much in common, not least the importance of their written work. They also shared a self-evident joy in vocabulary, and a predilection for satirical illustration. In fact, both were capable of tasty cartooning, similar in quality if not invention. While Perelman established himself as a popular cartoonist in the tight-budgeted Judge magazine, O'Nolan appeared briefly in the self-edited, short-lived Blather, which went into just six issues. Referring to his drawing in Cruiskeen Lawn, Myles boasts of the 'golden opinions, not to say encomia' won by his 'mastery of the old-time craft of the woodcut'. Similarly, Perelman's cartoons, those that weren't actually block prints touched with pen and ink, were mostly drawn in a style that parodied old woodcuts. Cartoonists may not make for great literature but S.J.'s picaresque masterpiece and best regarded work Westward Ha!, concerning his adventures in the company of the original Line King, Broadway caricaturist Al Hirschfeld, is as much a classic of its time as At Swim Two Birds.

Michael O'Nolan was transferred at regular intervals in the course of his work as a customs officer, and the O'Nolans also moved accordingly. In 1920, the family occupied a house two miles from Tullamore, called The Copper Beeches. The austere Offaly countryside was to provide Brian with the empty plain inhabited by The Third Policeman, an artless hive of inactivity in which a study such as the 'transmigration of molecules' phenomenon, involving the merging of molecules in a policeman's posterior with the molecules of his bicycle, might well thrive.

The O'Nolans moved to Dublin in 1923, and the non-Dubliner with the keenest sense of what makes Dubliners tick (those who aren't born thick, that is) had arrived, and he wasn't even held up in customs. Dublin has been known to give generously to the outsider. On the occasion of the first Bloomsday, O'Nolan would invoke Joyce as a non-Dubliner, one who was 'never at home'. Not so with Brian, the third of twelve children, who somehow found enough space at 4 Avoca Terrace, Blackrock, in which to write At Swim Two Birds.

Dubliners have always been among Europe's most avid moviegoers, and many have sat, as I did, through consecutive westerns in great Dublin art-houses, like The Corinthian, known colloquially as 'The Ranch'. Others may have had no choice but to wade through the aftermath of cattle-herding on the capital's streets en route to the North Circular Road's cattle market. And none of the above could be entirely surprised to encounter cowboys on the streets of O'Brien's Dublin.

Unsuccessful as a dramatist, O'Nolan achieved a vicarious triumph with the adaptation by Hugh Leonard of The Dalkey Archive, titled The Saints go Cycling In, which opened at the Gate Theatre in September 1965. It was to be his final comic turn.

Brendan Behan

If Anglo-Irish literature brings a connoisseur's eye to the world of *déclassé* Protestant aristocracy and the big house, Brendan Behan brings an insider's eye to a principal landmark of Dublin Bohemia, the public house. He drank, talked and brawled in spectacular fashion, played a self-styled wayward Irish wit to the gallery, ignored to his detriment the alcoholic waif within and became Dublin's most mythologised writer.

Like Oscar Wilde, Behan attracted, and generated, a massive mythology containing within it the seed of his downfall. In fact the two great wits of Irish letters sealed their fates by resolutely courting social disgrace. Both were victims of a self-inflicted syndrome, in which Oscar orchestrated his own artistic martyrdom while Brendan oversaw the dethronement of Behan the writer by Behan the drunken celebrity. With success came fame and Behan's appetite for public notice ruled his thinking, whether under lights or on air. As Wilde would have said 'There's only one thing worse than being talked about, and that's not being talked about'. A publicist initially for his own work, Behan developed a craving for what he described as his 'public ministry' which consumed him. By using the four letter word on BBC television's 'Malcolm Muggeridge Show' he became an overnight celebrity. Joan Littlewood's 1956 London production of *The Quare Fellow* had been a success, but subsequent appearances, with drink taken, on the 'nonsensical box' spread his fame far and wide. Accordingly he worked less, drank more, and came increasingly to see writing as a chore. His later books, dictated onto a tape recorder, were unconvincing and lacking in substance. Having settled for acclaim and glory, Behan, in an interview with the broadcaster Eamon Andrews, prophetically quoted John Keats 'God help the poor little famous'.

Family pressure, as much as the pressure of the past, had played its part when as a teenager he decided to visit perfidious Albion, intent on bombing same. He was arrested in 1939 in Liverpool, charged with possession of explosives and sentenced to three years in Borstal. Thus began an eventful prison career incorporating several sabbaticals at the pleasures of both Her Majesty's and the Irish government.In 1942 Behan published an article titled 'I Become a Borstal Boy' in *The Bell*. He manifested signs of a certain disregard for the guardians of the peace. When asked if he hated policemen,Behan replied 'I don't hate anybody, but I have never seen a situation so dismal that a policeman couldn't make it worse'. By the time his alcoholism took hold, his arrests were no longer for political reasons.

In 1955 he married Beatrice Ffrench-Salkeld, daughter of the painter Cecil Salkeld. A former student of Séan Keating, Salkeld defined his artistic principles as 'the minimum of form with the maximum of associations'. His mural 'The Triumph of Bacchus' can be seen at Davy Byrne's Pub in Duke Street. Beatrice was also an artist and her beautiful line drawings decorate Brendan's *Hold Your Hour and Have Another.*

When *The Hostage* premiered in London, in 1956, Brendan was reportedly too drunk to notice changes made by Joan Littlewood to adapt the play with topical references for an English audience. Kenneth Tynan predicted Behan would 'kick the English drama from the past into the present'. Never short of excuses Brendan made it clear that what was ruining his health was drinking to everyone else's.

Although he was one of nature's crowd pleasers and prey to what Anthony Cronin described as an 'insatiable desire for the favour of the generality', he indulged his wrath for 'kulchies and bogmen'. This required some perspicacity on Behan's part, as Dublin city is the home of the native and non-native in almost equal measure. If Brendan loved Dublin, at least half of Dublin reciprocated, by attending his funeral. When asked if he thought about dying, he had replied he'd rather be dead than think about it.

The Behans lived in 13 Russell Street, a strongly republican household, in a flat owned by Granny English who introduced Brendan to the tastes of porter and whiskey at an early age. In the mid 1930s, the family moved to 70 Kildare Road, in Kimmage where Brendan found himself surrounded, not just by strangers, but a southside people who 'ate their young'.

His confinements had become the raw material for his writing when in *Borstal Boy* he emoted 'caithfidh go bhfuil se go hiontach beith saor'.

Behan displayed a serious disdain for authority in his adolescent and adult life. Having shown a continuing disrespect towards two particular masters – the law of the land, and alcohol – he was put away, temporarily by one and permanently by the other.

With tongue in cheek, Brendan asserted he had only been to the country once and gone no further than County Wicklow, namely, Bray. In extremis, Brendan is said to have preferred to commune with nature in the air of St. Stephen's Green, which he particularly liked for its railings because they 'kept the kulchies out'.

Sources Noted and Quoted

Bowen, Elizabeth , *The Shelbourne,* Vintage, 2001

Calloway & Colvin, *The Exquisite Life of Oscar Wilde,* Orion, 1997

Coakley, Davis, *Oscar Wilde: The Importance of Being Irish,* Town House, 1994

Costello & De Kamp, *Flann O'Brien: An Illustrated Biography,* Bloomsbury, 1987

Cowell, John, *Where They Lived in Dublin,* O'Brien Press, 1980

Cox, Michael, *The Illustrated Le Fanu,* Equation, 1988

Cronin, Anthony, *Dead as Doornails,* Dolmen Press, 1976

Cronin, Anthony, *No Laughing Matter,* Grafton Books, 1989

Gibbon, Monk, *The Masterpiece and the Man,* Rupert Hart-Davis, 1959

Gillespie, Elgy, *The Liberties of Dublin,* E.& T. O'Brien, 1973

Goodman, Jonathan (ed.), *The Oscar Wilde File,* Allison & Busby, 1989

Haining & Tremayne, *The Un-Dead,* Constable, 1997

Hasegawa, Yoji, *A Walk in Kumamoto,* Global Oriental, 1997

Igoe, Vivien, *James Joyce's Dublin Houses,* Wolfhound Press, 1997

Krause, David, *Sean O'Casey and his World,* Thames & Hudson, 1976

Leatherdale, Clive, *The Origins of Dracula,* Desert Island Books, 1987

Ludlam, Harry, *A Biography of Dracula,* Foulsham, 1962

McCormack, W.J., *Sheridan le Fanu,* Lilliput Press, 1991

McCullough, Niall, *Dublin: An Urban History,* Anne Street Press, 1989

McLiammoir & Boland, *W. B. Yeats and his World,* Thames & Hudson, 1971

Marsh, Kate, *Writers and their Houses,* Hamish Hamilton, 1993

Miller, Elizabeth, *Dracula: Sense and Nonsense,* Desert Island Books, 2000

Minahan, John, *Samuel Beckett,* Secker & Warburg, 1995

Mulvey-Roberts, Marie, *The Handbook to Gothic Literature,* MacMillan Press, 1998

Murray, Paul, *A Fantastic Journey,* Japan Library, 1993

O'Connell, Derry, *The Antique Pavement,* An Taisce, 1975

O'Connor, Garry, *Sean O'Casey: A Life,* Hodder & Stoughton, 1988

O'Sullivan, Michael, *Brendan Behan: A Life,* Blackwater Press, 1997

Pearson, Peter, *The Heart of Dublin,* O'Brien Press, 2000

Ryan, John, *Remembering How We Stood,* Gill & MacMillan, 1975

Rosset, B., *Shaw of Dublin,* Pennsylvania State University Press, 1964

Shenfield, Margaret, *Bernard Shaw: A Pictorial Biography,* Thames & Hudson, 1962

Stephens, Edward, *My Uncle John,* Oxford University Press, 1974

Yeats, Michael B., *Cast a Cold Eye,* Blackwater Press, 1998